AMBRIDGE EXPOSED!

Jottings from Borchester Asylum

Barbara Williams
With additional material by
John O'Dwyer

CONTENTS

The Fairies of Ambridge*   5
How do we solve a problem like Roria?   7
    There was a young lady
    Jennifer's Lament
    Ambridge Vespers
    My Step-Father's Farm
The Grundy Love Triangle   13
    The Passionate Gamekeeper to His Love
    The Reply to the Gamekeeper
    The Emma Grundy Blues+
    The Waters of the Am**
Bert and MoiFreda   21
    Bert's Poem for the Townie Children
    To His Fat Wife
    The Silent Lovers of Ambridge
    MoiFreda's Mystery Men
Tiger and Pussycat   29
    Tiger and Pussycat+
    Ode to Nathan Booth
Religious Matters   33
    The Church With no Pews+**
    Misalliance in Ambridge
Other Ambridge Residents   39
    Kubla Khan comes to Ambridge
    Pip: Who was very boring and met an appropriate end
    Sabrina Thwaite
    The Ballad of Caroline Bone
The Truth about Uncle Rupert   49
    The real story of The Christmas Truce

+ available on Youtube
* by John O'Dwyer
** by Barbara Williams and John O'Dwyer

Acknowledgements

Thanks to Ian Sanderson for organising the Archers Anarchists
Ad alba vinceremo!

Thanks to John O'Dwyer for your contributions and the great music
Check him out on Youtube! Jjo2 .

Thanks to Jane, Richard and Graham for your help in getting this
thing printed.

Thanks to Matron and fellow inmates of Borchester Asylum
for your encouragement and friendship.

Introduction

This pitifully slim volume has been produced at the request of fellow inmates of Borchester Asylum. We all had a very nasty few weeks earlier this year when it looked as though our beloved Asylum might just fall into the hands of Borchester Land (or BL as we must now call it) and be converted into bijou apartments for Felpersham yuppies. But luckily the crested newts came to our rescue and BL's attention has turned to converting pack houses (whatever they are) and flogging farms off to tenants who don't seem to have noticed the credit crunch.

Borsetshire generally enjoys a strangely insulated position within the British Isles. It has its own micro-climate, a remarkably efficient if not miraculous health service (Borchester General specializes in Voice Transplants) and world events pass by unnoticed by the general population. It even moves from time to time, and buildings have a disconcerting habit of appearing from out of the blue then vanishing just as quickly as they appeared. A case in point is Sundial House, the school for children with special needs. This suddenly landed Tardis-like in the vicinity and, for a short time, Dave and Roof were completely obsessed with the place. No doubt the children were thrilled at the prospect of getting their sensory garden. Then all of a sudden it vanished! Hopefully it has ended up somewhere where the inhabitants have more commitment to their fundraising projects. Those children deserve better than Ambridge and the Archer family.

But I digress. Our creative writing therapy group has been fortunate enough to secure the services of Bert Fry as mentor and writing coach. He has even contributed a couple of his own poems to this collection. Being on the spot, we are able to see what really goes on in Ambridge and the vicinity, unlike those poor saps who are spoon fed snippets via the BBC. These misguided fools seem to believe the Archers is some kind of radio soap opera with scripts and actors. But through our little volume, we hope to give readers a glimpse of the sort of thing that really goes on in Ambridge.

Don't forget - the Archers are real - there IS no cast!
www.archersanarchists.com

NOTES ON SPELLING

As Anarchist-in-Chief Ian Sanderson points out in his excellent book "The Archers Anarchists A-Z" (available for a ridiculously small amount in Amazon's Market Place) we are reliant on the aural word and therefore have to spell as we find. Thus Brian is spelt as the name is pronounced by his wife ie. "Brine". William is always called "Wiwyerm" by his mother so his name is shortened to Wiw, and likewise Emma is "Aaremmur".

Anarchists have also given some Ambridge residents affectionate nick-names. Ruth has since her first operation been known as Flat Roof, though there has been some discussion as to whether she should now be Flat Roof Extension. Usually she is just shortened to Roof. David once made the mistake of telling Ken Ton how much he disliked being called Dave. This seemed an excellent reason to refer to him always by that name, so we do. It has saved many hours of discussion at Anarchist conventions as the spelling of Dave's name used to be the main topic on the agenda, and left little time for other business.

However, that is as nothing compared to the problem of Brine's 'little indiscretion'. His mother has always been referred to as Shove Horn, as it seemed so appropriate, and anyway nobody could spell her name properly. The boy is a big problem - and not just for Jennidahling. She seems to have settled on rhyming his name with Brewery, but that just doesn't do the name justice. So in the end anarchists have decided just to hit any combination of the R G H U A and I keys. The result does usually look like the sound of Joe expectorating but the informed reader will hopefully know who we mean.

FAIRIES OF AMBRIDGE

There are fairies at the bottom of our garden!
There are lots and lots – a proper fairy mob.
You pass the Grundys' shed
And you just keep straight ahead
I do so hope they've brought me a new job.

There's a little wood, with mice in it and muntjac,
There used to be a badger – he got shot.
But if anyone gets fired
They're very soon rehired
'Cos the fairies on the job are really hot.

There are fairies at the bottom of our garden!
They can magic up new cottages and homes.
The butterflies and bees
Make a lovely little breeze
As they flutter in among the Grundys' gnomes.

Did you know that they can cook a perfect pizza
When Ruth Archer chucks one in her microwave?
And at village cricket matches
Darrington drop all their catches.
O, there's not a situation they can't save.

There are fairies at the bottom of our garden!
They're so helpful to so many hopeless men –
Be it Alastair's online gambling
Or Jack Woolley's witless rambling
They make sure no harm should ever come to them.

And when Jill or Shula gets extremely tiresome,
Or when the Grundys and the Carters start to fight –
Whenever things get iffy
Fairies get there in a jiffy
And within a fortnight everything's put right.

John O'Dwyer

HOW DO WE SOLVE A PROBLEM LIKE RORIA?

There was a young lady called Shovehorn
With whom Brine was extremely lovelorn
But she said "Oh f*** it
Oi'me going to kick the bucket
Leaving Jenny to bring up the Shovespawn

Jennifer's lament

*On being confronted with the prospect of taking in
Shove and Brine's little bastard Rurraarugh*

Five years have passed, O husband mine
Since you met Shove and gave her one
But now I'm saying firmly Brine
I will not take your bastard son.

I know you took bastards of mine
And raised them up as if your own
But still I'm saying loudly Brine
I will not take your bastard son.

Shove may plead and cry and whine
And may well croak when all is done
But even then I'll insist Brine
I will not take your bastard son.

I'm getting on - past fifty nine! (well past actually)
I wanted retirement in the sun
Not more brats that aren't even mine
I will not take your bastard son.

And who's to say where is the line?
That Ruararaargh is the only one??
Knowing you, he isn't, Brine
I will not take your bastard son.

I've paid my dues and done my time
Now I'd like to have some fun
Sod off with Shove and Ruarrarrigh, Brine
I WILL NOT TAKE YOUR BASTARD SON!

Ambridge Vespers

Little boy kneels at the foot of the bed
Droops on the little hands little red head
Hush, hush, whisper who dares
Ruaruaurgh Aldridge is saying his prayers.

God bless Dieter, I know that's right
Wasn't it strange in the bath tonight
When the water was getting higher and higher
And Alice came in with an electric fire.

If I open my fingers a little bit more
I can see that weird Jennifer opening the door
Why is she holding that pillow so tight?
It's a peculiar way to say goodnight.

In my new room I lie in bed
And pull the duvet right over my head
And I shut my eyes and curl up small
And I wish I wasn't here at all.

Thanks a lot God for my lot in life
Ending up here with this creep and his wife
So if I survive it's no thanks to you
I'm joining The Coven like all kids here do.

My Step-Father's Farm
To the tune of My Grandfather's Clock

(Adam sings)

My step-father's farm is a real gold-mine
So that's why I'm staying put here.
I grit my teeth and I toe the line
Whilst I feed ewes and check on the deer.
I'm grumpy and cross and I act like I'm the boss
And I never apologise.
But I'll make sure I get the lot
When the old man dies.

(Debbie sings (over the phone))

My step-father's farm is worth loads of dosh
But I'm stuck here in Hun-gar-ee.
I talk on the phone and I spout lots of tosh
About agronomics and the CAP.
My eye's on the ball and I think I know it all
But I'm hoping for the star prize.
And I'll make sure I get the lot
When the old man dies.

(They duet)

Ten years we've grafted
We won't be shafted
We'll make sure we get the lot
When the old man dies.

11

(*Alice and Kate sing*)

Our family farm is where we both were born
So by rights it belongs to us.
And although it's to Africa we both have gorn
Still we won't give it up without a fuss.
One cottage apiece!! We are being fleeced!
So Ambridge will get a surprise.
An African orphanage we shall set up
When the old man dies.

(*Ruaarrrigh sings*)

My real daddy's farm is a great place to play
And me and Mousie have fun.
Mousie and me can't wait for the day
When it's all ours to have and to run.
It's going to be grand - on most of the land
Our Mousie World Theme Park will rise.
And that Bio-digester can go
When the old man dies.

(*Anarchists sing*)

Families brooding
Fighting and feuding.
We hope The Cat's Home gets the lot
When the old man dies.

THE GRUNDY LOVE TRIANGLE

<u>The Passionate Gamekeeper to his Love</u>

Come live with me and be my love
And we will all the pleasures prove
That Haydon Berrow, Jiggins Field
And all of Borsetshire can yield.

There will we stay in Casa Nueva
And sample delights of every flavour
Georgie, Jake and Mia too -
All happy as a pig in poo.

I will buy thee loads of stuff
And promise not to be too rough.
I'll take my boots off at the door
And try not to be such a bore.

And I shall cook and buy the wine
For thy delight this Valentine.
If these delights thy mind may move,
Then live with me and be my love.

The Reply to the Passionate Gamekeeper

If Casa Nueva were in town
And Georgie didn't get me down
Then your words might well make me move
To live with thee and be thy love.

But the countryside gives me the creeps
The loneliness just makes me weep.
You seem to have no time for me
I've only Joe for company.

So thanks for buying all the stuff.
I'll tell you when I've got enough.
A holiday might be rather fun
I'd really like some winter sun.

But living in the country's out.
Of that there's not a single doubt.
So sorry Wiw, but I can't move
To live with thee and be thy love.

The Emma Grundy Blues

Traditional blues from the Am Delta region

Woke up this mornin' in a strange bedroom
I had a bad feelin' full o' dread and gloom
I'm stuck here with Fallon Rogers in a B&B in Woolacombe
No lead in my pencil, impotence was my doom.

The woman I love, she treated me so bad
Loved me but wed my brother, that made me feel quite sad
Then she had wee Georgie, told me I was his dad
Did you ever get the feelin' that you've been had.

Well, we set up home together in a little caravan
I told her she was my woman and I would always be her man
I said "I'll look after you and Georgie, I'll do the best I can"
And at the time, it seemed a pretty good plan.

But then my no good brother demanded a paternity test
He said "Oi'm George's faarver , I can look after him best"
Turned out he was right, well I might just have guessed
Is it any wonder I'm feelin' slightly depressed.

And then my baby left me she went back to her dad and
mum
I went on a bender just to make my brain go numb
I turned to drugs and boozin' and became a no good bum
Well lookin' back, that sure was pretty dumb.

Well then Oliver, he saved me, he picked me up off the floor
He said "Boy you done with drinkin' don't you take them
drugs no more.
You and me we'll start a milk round, just what Ambridge
folks are waitin' for"
Organic milk delivered right to your door.

Life was lookin' pretty good I had a job that suited me
And from all my addictions made a full recovery
But then disaster hit us, and those cows, they all got TB
Even those badgers, they've got it in for me.

So now I see my brother he's doin' pretty fine
Got some cash from Aunty Hilda some of that should've been
mine
Looks like he's gettin' back with Emma while me, I can't stop
cryin'
I tell myself I don't care, but I know I'm lyin'.

Last night I had a problem couldn't think of an excuse
Why I couldn't shag that Fallon though she played fast and
loose
It's cos I'm thinkin' of another woman......
I got those Emma Grundy
Those Emma Grundy Bluuueeees.

The Waters of the Am

I can't believe you've gone back to my brother
After all the pain he put you through
He takes from me one thing after another
And I am left alone and feelin' blue.
You know that I was faithful and devoted
I loved you Emma dear right from the start
But now the die is cast, and our love is in the past
And the waters of the Am will never heal my broken
heart.

You left me and I thought I'd die of sorrow
My world collapsed just like a house of cards
I didn't think the sun would rise tomorrow
My heart of glass was broken into shards.
You took away my dearest little Georgie
Our happy family life was blown apart
My wrists I could have cut in that cursèd shepherds
hut
And the waters of the Am will never heal my broken
heart.

O its fresh waters flow
As my salt tears fall down
And one day I'll go
Down to that river and drown.

I thought that love once more had come a'callin'
When on a bus a girl I chanced to meet
Her smile and sparklin' blue eyes had me fallin'
But behind the smile was cruelty and deceit.
Just for a while I thought she could replace you
But we were actors playin' out a part
If you and George came back, my life would be on
track
But the waters of the Am will never heal my broken
heart.

But now that you have gone back to my brother
I see that there's no chance of a reprieve
Even though you are wee Georgie's mother
Your fate is sealed and justice you'll receive.
For I am judge and jury, priest and hangman
And I have ice where once I had a heart
Now the end is nigh and both of you must die
And 'neath the waters of the Am you'll never need to
be apart.

O its fresh waters flow
As my salt tears fall down
And soon you'll both go
Down to that river and drown.

BERT
AND
MOIFREDA

Bert's Poem for the Townie Children

Written on the occasion of the visit of some Townie ruffians to Brookfield Farm.

Welcome to Brookfield
A mixed sort of farm
If you are quite careful
You'll come to no harm.

Here's David the master
Of whom it is said
He once shot a badger
And killed it stone dead.

Here's Roof, she's his missus
Looks after the cows
And also the cow men
When conscience allows.

Here are the children
Pip, Ben and Josh
They're mad about fishing
And surprisingly posh.

This is a cow
From which we get milk
We also get beef
From a different ilk (of cow that is).

This is a sheep
From which we get wool
We also get lamb
To eat, as a rule.

This is a hen
From which we get eggs
And also roast chicken
For strong arms and legs.

This is a tractor
On which I do plough
I do competitions
And win them somehow.

This is a field
In which we grow crops
Maize, wheat and potatoes
The work never stops.

So now you can see
From where comes your food
Sod off back to London
You ignorant brood!

Bert Fry
I like to think my poem gave those townie kids a real insight into rural life.

To His Fat Wife: by Bert Froi

Had we but time enough and space
This fatness would be no disgrace.
We would sit down and think till late
How you could lose your excess weight.
By the gentle Am we'd think
Of all the diets. Food and drink
You must forego and meals refuse
Till the removal of the pews.
My vegetables, love, I'll grow
And salad crops I'll gladly sow.
But to cakes and biscuits, just say no
Or vaster than empires you will grow.
For at my back I always hear
Time's winged chariot drawing near.
And excess weight I greatly fear
Can shorten your life by many a year.
The Bull's a fine and friendly pub
And people like your home-cooked grub
But you my love must show restraint
And have the virtues of a saint.
To Ambridge Fat Club you'll away
And play some sport, while you still may
Calories out must well exceed
Calories in for you to succeed.
Thus though it may be very grim
Yet I will make moiFreda slim.

<u>The Silent Lovers of Ambridge</u>
A tribute to Freda Froi and Neville Booth.

Theirs was a silent passion
Both were held in thrall
As wordlessly their eyes met
Across the village hall.

Freda, mute as ever,
But full of slimline zest
Neville in his plimsolls
Joggers and string vest.

Though words remained unspoken
Both quietly understood
The strength of their desire
Resist it though they should.

They met again on Sunday
And by St. Stephen's door
He softly touched her shoulder
Her look demanded more.

Their mutual gaze spoke volumes
Though not a sound was heard
The love that dare not speak at all
Needs not a single word.

After Sid and Jolene
Roof and Soapy Sam
Thank God for silent lovers
Canoodling by the Am.

MoiFreda's Mystery Men

Regular listeners to events in Ambridge may recall that, having bullied MoiFreda into going to the Fat Club, he then got very jealous when she actually lost weight and smartened herself up a bit. He was convinced she had a lover- little did he know........

Twas on a Monday morning
George Clooney came to call.
Bert was helping Robert Snell
He'd gone to Ambridge Hall.
I put George through his paces
We had a marvellous day
But by six he was exhausted
So I sent him on his way.

Twas on a Tuesday morning
Brad Pitt came around.
Bert was at Lower Loxley
With some photographs he'd found.
Brad was acrobatic
His antics made me groan
But then he put his back out
And I had to send him home.

Twas on a Wednesday morning
Johnny Depp arrived.
Bert had gone to Oxford
On an errand I'd contrived.
Johnny brought his pirate gear
We had some salty fun
But then Vanessa called him
And at five he had to run.

Twas on a Thursday morning
Colin Firth dropped by.
Bert had gone to Brookfield
I didn't ask him why.
Colin dived into the Am
In his frilly shirt
But he had to go home after
As he said his chilblains hurt.

Twas on a Friday morning
Sean Bean rang the bell.
Bert had gone to see a friend
Who wasn't very well.
I was Lady Constance
With flowers in my hair
But Sean kept all his clothes on
Which wasn't really fair.

On Saturday and Sunday
Nobody came at all.
So twas on a Monday morning
That George Clooney came to call.

TIGER AND PUSSYCAT

<u>Tiger and Pussycat</u>

Tiger and Pussycat had a row
He really had got her goat
So she took her bags and plenty of fags
And her beautiful mink fur coat.

And at the Bull as the pints she pulled
She wailed from behind the bar:
'Oh faithless Tiger, oh Tiger my love
What a two timing bastard you are, you are, you are....
What a two timing bastard you are'.

Then Tiger came in and bought her a gin
He said 'Pour us a pint and we'll talk'.
She said 'Are you sorry, for causing such worry?
Admit it is you who's at fault'.

But Tiger denied he had ever lied
And said he was not to blame.
'Oh lovely Pusscat, oh Pusscat my love,
Annabel's not my new flame, new flame, new flame....
Annabel's not my new flame.

Pusscat said 'You had better obey to the letter
My demand'. Tiger said 'Not on your nellie!'
So she sent him away, and the very next day
He's with Annabel down Botticellis.

And Puss looks up to the stars above
While Jennifer gets her pen.
And hand in hand by the edge of the Am
They lament their faithless men, thless men, thless men.....
They lament their faithless men.

This anonymous verse was written in a Valentines card:
The fact that Lilian was separated from Matt and looking for love
is of course completely coincidental.

Oh Nathan Booth, Nathan Booth
Your name a savage breast would soothe.
You are more handsome and more fair
Than sluglips Barry (with the hair).

Your conversation may be minimal
Your record just a little criminal
Yet it's for you I have a yen
Oh bravest of the Ambridge men.

It's true your eyes are somewhat crossed
And half your teeth seem to be lost.
But still it is for you I pine
To be my one true Valentine.

But if by chance you do refuse
To let me be your love and muse.
I'll have to cast care to the Devil
And make do with your Uncle Neville.

RELIGIOUS MATTERS

The Church with no Pews

Anarchists followed with great concern Alan's campaign to rid St. Stephen's of its lovely old pews in order to make the church a 'community resource'. We'd always been under the impression that was the function of the Village Hall, whereas the Church was for worshipping God, but we bow to the Vicar's greater knowledge. In the event, he was outvoted but one can imagine how things might have been.......

In Ambridge they're wailing, their teeth they do gnash
St Stephen's is worse than a bank with no cash.
It's almost as sad as a pub with no booze
To stand in the aisle of a church with no pews.

Bert's banging on like a broken LP,
How a church you can't sit in is a calamity,
You can't creep to the back for a bit of a snooze,
You must stand in the aisle of a church with no pews.

Shula has just had a fit of despair,
'Cause St Steve's now accessible for a wheelchair.
She comforts herself with a pint of Chartreuse,
As Jim rolls down the aisle of a church with no pews.

For Pilates you can lie on a nice rubber mat,
For yoga you can squat with your feet up your back.
You must stand through the sermon, or possibly cruise
Up and down in the aisle of a church with no pews.

There's French and macramé, maintaining your car
There's Scotch country dancing and flute and guitar
There's barber's shop singers and rhythm and blues
All jostling for space in the church with no pews.

There's salsa and tango, photography and Dutch
Reflexology, astrology and healing by touch.
The flower arrangers form orderly queues
And the Satanists now meet in the church with no
pews.

Rehearsals are held for the next village play
And Lynda shows Titcombe and Eileen the way
Jerry Springer the Opera is bound to amuse
The Christians of Ambridge in the church with no
pews.

Mabel's come back and now cooks up stock
In the vestry soup kitchen she tends her new flock
The drug addicts know they have nothing to lose
So turn up in droves at the church with no pews.

The Bull's quiet too now the pews have all gone
But Eddie's speakeasy is second to none
There's cider on tap and all kinds of booze
Available to buy at the church with no pews.

At night a red light appears over the door
And a mattress goes down on the now empty floor,
In the phone box a small card announces the news -
Aar'Emmur's found a job in the church with no pews.

Multi-faith worship's the order of the day
Now that the pews have been taken away
Hindus and Buddhists, Muslims and Jews
And the Jedi all meet in the church with no pews.

The poor village hall stands deserted and cold
For no-one goes there now the pews have been sold.
They're all in St. Stephens since getting the news
That it's cheaper to meet in the church with no pews.

The old congregation have melted away
Since the pews went on ebay there's nowhere to pray
They've either turned Chapel, or got atheist views
(thanks Professor Jim!)
Leaving Alan to manage the church with no pews.

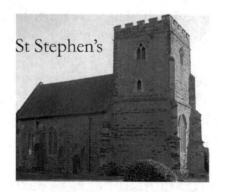

St Stephen's

Members of all denominations and none welcome!

Misalliance in Ambridge

Christians, they usually worship just one god
And many other faiths do just the same.
But some have many deities and worship the whole lot.
Hindus are one group that I could name.

In Ambridge there's a Christian flock with Alan at its head
Though some folk have their doubts about his views.
There's also a solicitor, a Hindu born and bred.
They met, love blossomed in amongst the pews.

Said the Christian vicar to the resident Hindu
"Oh let us be married, I've prayed I will win you
Please accept my offer, we can't live in sin, you
'll be happy with me" said the vicar to the Hindu.

To Grandmother Mabel it came as a blow.
"The Hindus" she said "are just not in the know.
They don't understand, our God's is the True Word.
The only solution is she must convert."

Said Oosha the Hindu to Alan the vicar
"Your ma-in-law really does get on my wick. Our
Love only seems to make her quite sick. Our
Happiness is blighted" said Oosha to the vicar.

Satya said Oosha would be condemned.
Outcast from the family, damned without end.
There was no salvation, no saving grace.
"This marriage" she said "must never take place".

Said the Christian vicar to his affianced Hindu
"It seems that our families all are agin, do
we care if they think we're committing a sin? Do
we heck, we'll marry anyhow" said the vicar to the Hindu.

Together they left on the very next day.
They travelled to Scotland on Virgin Railway.
They both spurned their churches and opted for Wicca.
"Happy Pagans we'll be" said the Hindu and the Vicar.

OTHER AMBRIDGE RESIDENTS

KUBLA KHAN COMES TO AMBRIDGE

IN GRUNDY'S FIELD DID KUBLA KHAN
A STATELY PLEASURE DOME DECREE
WHERE AM THE SACRED RIVER RUNS
AND CLARRIE'S SELLING HOME MADE BUNS
AND STRAWBERRIES FOR TEA.

THREE ACRES OF NEGLECTED GROUND
WITH STRAGGLY THORN HEDGE GIRDLED ROUND
AND THERE A POLE BARN RED WITH RUST
WHERE MANY A MOONING GARDEN GNOME
STANDS IN THE CORNER GATHERING DUST
WAITING TO BE FOUND A HOME.

AND HERE A BADLY PUT UP SHED
WITH RAMPANT IVY COVERÈD
AND ALL SHOULD CRY BEWARE BEWARE!
BEWARE THE COMPOST STACKED IN THERE.

AND CAKED IN MUD GRUNTING WITH PLEASURE
A BERKSHIRE SOW NAMED BARBARELLA
IN HER PEN SHE GRUBS AROUND
FOR SCRAPS OF FOOD LEFT ON THE GROUND
OR ANY OTHER HIDDEN TREASURE.

A SAVAGE PLACE WITH DOCK AND NETTLE
DANDELION AND BUTTERCUP CREEPING,
BROKEN CHINA, DISCARDED KETTLE
UNIDENTIFIED BITS OF METAL
FROM ANCIENT TRACTOR, BLACK OIL SEEPING,
AND MIDST THIS MESS, THIS MAD BAZAAR
A VOICE WAS HEARD RAISED FROM AFAR
"FIFTEEN QUID TO PARK THE CAR!!"

KUBLA LOOKED ON IN DESPAIR
AND TOOK HIS PLEASURE DOME ELSEWHERE.

40

Pip

Who was extremely boring and met a suitably eco-friendly fate

Pip was such a frightful bore
She'd have you snoring on the floor
The kids at school would run away
Whenever she came round to play
All her little would be chums
Would piteously beg their dads and mums
"Please don't invite her round our house
All she talks about is cows".
Of school work she had little clue
And Van Gogh's ear for music too.
In spite of all this evidence
Her grandparents (who had no sense)
Thought "Here's a high achiever who'll
Do well at the Cathedral School."
But Dave and Flat Roof said "Ooh nooo
To the bog standard comp she'll go.
There she'll learn to socialise
And mix with kids from Meadow Rise.
For herself she'll learn to fend
She'll maybe even find a friend."
But unlikely though it may seem
Her boringness got more extreme
Instead of shops and girly prattle
She'd spend her weekends judging cattle.
Whilst others talked of boys and fashion
Skylarks nesting was her passion.
She'd hector folk on population
And urged an end to copulation

"We must act now to save the planet!"
And as for flying, well she'd ban it.
But villagers had had enough
Of all her sanctimonious guff.
Rather than let feelings fester
They stuck her in the poo digester.
She met an end much to her taste -
Pip became recycled waste.

Sabrina Thwaite

Little is known about this Ambridge resident, other than the fact that she takes care of herself and usually looks glamorous. This is a deliberate ploy on her part to conceal her true identity.

Sabrina Thwaite's a Mystery Girl: she's called double-O Four
For she's an undercover cop who must uphold the Law.
To Ambridge folk she's lightweight, she's just Sabrina Fair
But wherever there's a scene of crime - *Sabrina Thwaite is there*!

Sabrina, Sabrina, there's no-one like Sabrina,
Although she's witnessed lots of crime, nobody's ever seen her.
She'll melt into the background, she's a master of disguise,
She's infiltrated Netherborne Hall as well as Meadow Rise.
Wherever there's a burglar, lurking on a stair -
One thing you can be sure of, *Sabrina will be there*!

Sabrina is a fitness freak, she's fairly tall and slim;
You'd know her if you saw her, she's often down the gym.
Her eyes are green and cat-like, her hair is chestnut brown;
She drives a little sports car whilst zipping round the town.
Her clothes are all designer, she won't have second best;
Just putting out the dustbins, she's immaculately dressed.

Sabrina, Sabrina, there's no-one like Sabrina,
And when it comes to fighting crime, there's nobody who's keener.
Wherever there's a drug dealer, she'll track him to his lair -
And summon the Constabulary. Thank God *Sabrina's there*!

But Ambridge is her special brief, and she is on the case.
(She says she's never come across so criminal a place.)
Armed robbery, rape and arson, attempted fratricide,
Drug addiction, gambling, they've all got things to hide.
And all those ruthless killers had better just beware -
The truth will be discovered now that *Sabrina's there*.

She's a specialist in rural crime, a credit to the force.
She's trained with DI Barnaby and knew Inspector Morse.
She knows behind the cottage doors pure evil could be lurking,
And underneath a smug façade a criminal mind is working.
The deaths have been too numerous - the motives seem quite plain,
You only have to ask yourself who has the most to gain?
So next time a rich relative sits dozing in a chair,
Before a cushion smothers them, *Sabrina will be there*!

Sabrina, Sabrina, there's no-one like Sabrina,
She never lets the strain and stress disturb her calm demeanour.
With mayhem all around her she always keeps her cool,
Silently observing the Ambridge Ship of Fools.
The Archer women seem to her particularly vicious -
To lose one husband might be sad - to lose two is suspicious.
But hopefully it won't be long before they're serving time,
And all thanks to Sabrina Thwaite, the Scourge of Ambridge Crime!

The Ballad of Caroline Bone

I tell the tale of Caroline Bone
A pearls and twinset sort of Sloane
Descended from the ruling class
Her dulcet tones were pure cut glass.
Her education was expensive
Her knowledge of etiquette extensive
Her cooking skills beyond compare
She rode to hounds with skill and flair.
In truth there was just one thing wrong
She couldn't keep her knickers on.
She gained some jolly useful knowledge
Whilst still at Cheltenham Ladies College
And had a measure of success
With the nearby SAS.
And when to Surrey she did move
Her cordon bleu skills to improve
The Sandhurst men proved quite a draw
And often turned up at her door.
Thence to Henley for the Season
Looking round she saw no reason
To stick with men in uniform.
In Henley it was quite the norm
To have an oarsman by one's side.
Indeed it was a source of pride.
And so she duly paid her sub
And worked through the Leander Club.
At Glyndebourne music stirred her soul
Musicians then became her goal.
The orchestra won her affection
But she only had the woodwind section.

So to Ambridge and The Bull
Caroline was on the pull!
A husband was her main ambition
Here was a woman on a mission.
But, to dispel any doubt
She thought she'd better try some out.
Doctors, lawyers, vets and vicars
Businessmen with dodgy tickers
Ingenu or seedy lecher
Brian Aldridge, Derek Fletcher
Pensioner or callow youth
She had Nathan AND Neville Booth
Bald men, ginger, dark or fair
Sluglips Barry (with the hair)
Builders, farmers, pig- or cowman
Sid Perks (one night in the Ploughmans)
Nigel in his ice cream van
Herbert the milk tanker man
Prince or pauper, Lord or woodman
Fat Paul and Sir Sidney Goodman
Who liked to chase her through the shrubbery
Wearing something strange and rubbery.

Finally she settled upon
The millionaire Guy Pemberton
Folk in Ambridge scratched their heads
Why was it him she chose to wed?
They couldn't work it out at all
He wasn't handsome, clever, tall
In fact had nothing much to please
And suffered from chronic heart disease

Six months later he departed.
Caroline was broken hearted.
Before she'd moved in for the kill
She'd made quite sure he'd changed his will.
But the bastard let her down
On his last journey into town.
A codicil had sealed her fate
She only got half the estate.

Whilst waiting for another sucker
She got a lodger in to help her
A lusty youth named William Grundy
He used to help her every Sunday.
Eagerly he'd ring her bell
He did the jobs extremely well.
Finally she struck Sterling gold
Another millionaire! Quite old
Florid face, inclined to wheeze
All the signs of heart disease!
Shouldn't be too long to wait
Until he met his deadly fate.
And so she plays a waiting game
But Oliver is in the frame
If there is too much delay
She means to send him on his way.
One day they will find him dead
Stretched out naked on the bed
Beside him boots, hard hat and whip
A happy smile upon his lips
A tally ho his final breath
As Caroline rides him to death.

THE TRUTH ABOUT UNCLE RUPERT

The Christmas Truce: and Uncle Rupert's part in it.

"Mein liebes weibchen

I have such a strange story to tell you, you will not believe it. It was Christmas Eve- a beautiful cold, starry night and we were huddled together in our trench thinking of our loved ones back home, and of the futility of this accursed war. I thought of you mein liebchen and of little Friedrich and Lilli and how excited they would be this Heiligabend. I hoped that they would not forget their father fighting for the Fatherland in this god forsaken place.

The guns had fallen silent as midnight approached and we could hear sounds from the enemy trenches. For one moment we even thought we could hear the strains of 'Stille Nacht" drifting across no mans land. We listened enchanted and were just about to join in, when suddenly a gorilla tumbled into our trench on top of us! Mein liebchen, you can imagine our surprise! We were even more amazed when we discovered the gorilla was clutching a half empty bottle of champagne! We soon realised that things weren't all they seemed when the gorilla swore loudly in English and asked us the way to Piccadilly. He sat up with difficulty and began singing a song I didn't recognise, but seemed to be about a lady called Nellie Dean. We were so amazed, it was like a Christmas apparition!

Well, it being Christmas Eve, and the guns being silent, we called across to the enemy:

"Tommy!"

They called back

"'Allo?"

We called to them:

"There is a gorilla in our trench singing a song about Nellie Dean. He has a bottle of champagne."

This was greeted with muffled whispers- they seemed to be having some sort of discussion. Then they called back.

"He's ours, but you can keep him if you like. He's a Christmas present".

Well, we weren't sure what to do. It was most kind of Tommy to give us their singing gorilla, but we were not at all sure we could keep him, so we called back.

"Tommy! Thank you so much for the gift of the gorilla, but we're not sure we can keep him. We'll send him over to you.

Back came their reply.

"Nah - you keep him. He's useful. He's a stretcher bearer."

We found this hard to believe and decided Tommy was as the English say, pulling our legs, so we responded.

"We have stretcher bearers - and we're not sure how to look after gorillas. What do they eat?"

The reply came across no mans land.

"Well that one doesn't so much eat as drink - but he will drink anything."

"Even so Tommy, we thank you but please let us escort him back to you. Shall we meet half way?"

And with that, a tin hat appeared above the trench and Tommy waved across.

"Don't shoot - I'm coming to get him"

So Fritz and I each put an arm under the arms of the gorilla and pulled him to his feet. His response was to hit Fritz over the head with the champagne bottle, shouting out

"I say get off! Don't you know who I am? I know the chief constable of Borsetshire personally."

But then his knees gave way and it was easy to drag him out of the trench and across no mans land to where Tommy was waiting with a group of his comrades. They tried one last time to persuade us to keep the gorilla, but finally they gave in and took him back to their own trench.

By now of course it was Christmas morning, and none of us had the desire to recommence fighting, so I said to Tommy

"How about a game of football?"

51